Amazing You

Fortune Telling

Teresa Moorey

a division of Hodder Headline Limited

About the series

Amazing You is our stunning new Mind Body Spirit
series. It shows you how to make the most of your life
and boost your chances of success and happiness.
You'll discover some fantastic things about you and
your friends by trying out the great tips and fun
exercises. See for yourself just how amazing you
can be!

Titles in the series
Astrology
Crystals
Dreams
Face and Hand Reading
Fortune Telling
Graphology
Numerology
Psychic Powers
Spells

About the author

Teresa Moorey is a counsellor, astrologer and author of over forty books on witchcraft and related subjects. She is also a mother of four children aged 6–23. Teresa writes for *Mizz* magazine and *Here's Health*, and is the author of *Spell Bound: The Teenage Witch's Essential Wicca Handbook* and *Witchcraft: A Beginner's Guide*. She has written *Crystals*, *Fortune Telling*, *Graphology* and *Spells* in the *Amazing You* series.

✳ ★ ✳ ★

Contents

INTRODUCTION

Foretelling the future

Is it really possible to foretell the future? Do some people have a special gift for this? The answer is yes, to both questions, and the good news is that you can develop your talents and ability to take a peek into what's going to happen.

Some people say it's crazy to think you can predict something because if it hasn't happened then it hasn't happened. But life isn't that simple. Some scientists state that it is possible to travel in time, although we don't yet know how to – at least not in our bodies. In the mind however, it is another matter entirely. Your mind is capable of so many things that you have not yet discovered. Some people say that the human race is evolving and that we are all slowly developing

psychic powers. Others say that psychic powers
were something everyone had many thousands

of years ago, before we talked ourselves out
of them by being 'logical', and that they are
within us, just waiting to be rediscovered.

Whatever the case may be, there are amazing
abilities within you, and you just need to learn
how to discover them.

In this book we shall be looking at several old
ways of foretelling the future and boosting your
psychic powers. Is there some
magic in these 'old ways'? Yes,
and no. When something has been
done in the same way, or a way
like it, for many hundreds of years, then it does
have a kind of magic about it – it is as if the
spirit pathways have been opened up.

But however old something is, however many
people have used it in the past, it will be no good
at all unless you bring your intuition into what
you do. And with your intuition in place it will
not matter very much if you don't do it 'quite

right'. All the methods of fortune telling
are made for one thing – to get your

★ ✳ ★

subconscious mind in gear, to get your instincts to work.

After you have tried out the different methods of fortune telling in this book, it is quite likely that you will decide that one works better for you than the others. This is because it has the right triggers for your subconscious. Something about it helps you get into that frame of mind where you are open and can easily sense things.

How should you approach your fortune telling? The best way is to be playful, but respectful. When you are relaxed and enjoying yourself you are far more likely to pick things up. However, it is also important to be sensible and to realize that you are dealing with something that is powerful and special.

And what about scary predictions? Obviously we all know bad things do occasionally happen, but you will be asking questions about your daily life, to do with lads, school and friends, and there just isn't anything THAT bad that can happen there! Use your imagination positively – always look for the good in what you see.

Finally, the great news about the future is that it is yours to shape. Scientists tell us that there may be many alternate dimensions, many different 'realities' that branch off at every instant where we make a decision. So always remember that any future that you see isn't set in stone. You have free will and you have choices. One of the wonderful things about fortune telling is that it can make your choices clearer for you, giving you insight and putting you more in control of your life.

So take a peek into your future – and make your dreams come true!

CHAPTER ONE

Dealing destiny

You can tell your fortune remarkably well with an ordinary pack of playing cards, once you get wised up. People have used these for hundreds of years to answer questions about life. In the days before TV they were used all the time to play games, too. Like Tarot cards, they are believed to have been brought from Egypt or India, by gypsies. (Tarot cards have dramatic pictures on them that you can deal out to find answers to questions. Each of the cards has a special meaning.) Lots of families had their own after-dinner fortune teller – maybe your own Nan's Mum was a Mystic Meg, and the skill could have passed down to you!

You can use any pack of cards for fortune

telling, and there is sure to be at least
one hanging about in your house, so this
is a good method if you're short of cash.
However, you might still like the idea of getting a
special pack, just for fortune telling. If you decide
to do this you may like to dedicate your pack to
the powers of good before using them. Just light
a lavender joss stick and pass your cards through
the sweet smoke, saying, 'May these cards be
cleansed of all that is negative, leaving only
good within them'. Store them in their own
special bag or box and only get them out
when you are using them for fortune telling.
It is best not to let anyone else touch your pack,
except when you are doing a reading for them –
and then you might like to re-cleanse your cards
afterwards. Of course, you could have a pack
between the whole gang, to use at sleepovers
and get-togethers, if you like.

When you are ready to use the cards,
sit still for a while, holding your pack
quietly between your palms. Perhaps
light a candle (if you are allowed) to get
a dreamy, relaxed feeling inside. Then shuffle your
pack gently, while you get your question straight

in your mind. When you are ready, start dealing your cards. If you are doing this with a friend and she wants to ask a question, she should cut the pack before dealing. Here are some questions you can ask, and answers to interpret.

★★ YES/NO QUESTIONS

You can use this method to help you whenever you aren't sure what decision to make. This could be anything from: 'Will tomorrow be a good day to ask Mum about those new trainers?' to 'Should I tell that lad I think he's cool?'. You can also use it to find out things like: 'Can I trust my friend's opinion?' or 'Does he really like me?'. But remember, all the cards can ever do is help your own intuition. Use your common sense and don't take it too seriously.

First shuffle the cards, hold them in your left hand and close your eyes. Mentally ask your question, making sure it is very clear. Now cut the pack and look at the card you have turned up.

It's very simple! If your card is a heart or a diamond, then the answer is 'yes', if it's a club or a spade then it's 'no'. But we all know there are degrees of 'no' or 'yes'. The strongest answer is an Ace – a very definite 'yes' or 'no'. After that comes a King, Queen, Jack and then down the numbers with Two being so weak as to be almost a 'maybe'.

If you aren't happy with the answer, don't let it bother you. You can find a way to make things work out. What can you learn from this? Do you need to look at things in a different way? What is really best for you? Take charge of your life and see if you can find a way that suits you.

✦ ★ DEALING WITH HOLIDAY TIME

It can be hard to get the best from the holidays. Being with your folks can be stressful and sometimes it feels like there's no pleasing Mum or Dad. Use this method to get clues from the cards.

First take out all the picture cards. Then pick out a Queen to fit your Mum and a King for your Dad. If they are blond choose Diamonds, Hearts

for light brown hair, Clubs for dark hair and
 Spades for black hair. Lay your chosen cards
down, face up. Hold the rest of the pack
and close your eyes. Ask to be shown the
best way of getting your Mum or Dad on
side. Shuffle the cards and deal one card on top
of the Queen and another on top of the King.

If the card you've dealt is a Diamond, then
Mum or Dad want you to be switched on and
alert. No sitting in a corner with your nose buried
in a magazine! It will be best to offer to help out
with plans, make sensible suggestions and even do
some housework too!

If the card is a Heart then it seems
like they want you to be understanding
and kind. Help out with your little
brother or sister, make your Mum a
cuppa and pass food round at mealtimes.

If the card is a Club then money could be
a problem. Show you understand the value of
money by working to get extra cash outside the
home, doing jobs for your Nan and maybe car-
 washing for neighbours – although
obviously you'll be sensible and only ask
people you already know. Make the most

of cheaper outings by being cheerful and having a giggle.

If the card is a Spade then hard work is on the cards! You may be asked to help with decorating or gardening. With Spades what counts is your attitude, so make sure it's positive and in the end you'll reap the rewards.

✶✶ GREAT MATES

Here's a game to play with your best friend. You'll learn a lot about each other, so make sure you're ready for it!

First you each choose a Queen or a Jack to represent you, using the same guidelines given in the previous section for picking a card to represent your folks. Place the card on the table, face up. Now take it in turns to hold the cards and ask the question: 'What's great about my mate?'. Take out one card and put it on top of your friend's card. If the card's a Diamond you

think she's a great laugh and generous too – there's always something happening round

her. If it's a Heart you love her because
she's always kind and caring; you can
trust her and she always gives you a
hug if you are stressed out or upset. If it's a Club
you like the way she shares her clothes and stuff
and encourages you to be the best at whatever
you try to do. If it's a Spade you think being with
her makes you look cool because she's really clever
and quick, although sometimes she can be hard
work! The higher the card the better, with Aces
highest of all.

For your next question ask what you hope for
from the friendship. A Diamond means you hope
to meet lots of new people; Hearts mean you
want to be friends forever; Clubs that she'll
help you sort out your room and have lots of
fabulous ideas about what you can do
together; and Spades you hope some of her
savvy will rub off on you!

The last question is: 'What can you give?'. If
it's Diamonds you cheer her up and share your
stuff; if it's Hearts it's a big hug; if Clubs
then you can give good advice and make
her feel great; if it's Spades you get her
out of scrapes – or into one!

★★ LEARNING ABOUT THE LADS

If you want to know a bit more about that
gorgeous lad, this is how you go about it. First
take out the Kings and Jacks. Put the Kings to
one side and pick a Jack to fit him according
to his hair colour – Diamond blond, Heart light
brown, Club dark brown and Spade black. Place
this Jack face up on the table. Shuffle the rest of
the pack, close your eyes and ask: 'What can he
give me?'. Deal a card on top of the Jack. If it's
a Diamond he'll make you chuckle and
he could be very generous; if it's a
Heart it looks like you're getting close;
if it's a Club he'll show you a good
time and he'll want to make an
impression; and if it's a Spade he could help you,
but he's got a secret.

   Now shuffle again and ask: 'What does he like
about me?'. A Diamond means he thinks you're
gorgeous and you always look sassy; a Heart says
he thinks you're the warmest girl he's ever met

and he trusts you; a Club means you're a good friend and great to go places with; and a Spade says he thinks you're cool but he's scared!

Shuffle again and ask: 'What's the best way to get his attention?'. If you deal a Diamond, keep wearing that cool outfit; if it's a Heart it could be safe to say how you feel; if it's a Club hang out with him to get closer and if it's a Spade be understanding – he could need some support.

And if you deal a Queen at any time, watch out – there's another girl involved in some way, so stay cool!

Clued-up on the cards

The ways just described of laying the cards out are simple and focused on only one thing. However, if you want to get to know the cards properly, you need to be aware of what the four suits mean, and have some idea what each single card means. Then you can do a spread about almost anything, or

ask a general question such as: 'What
are the next few days going to
bring?'; 'What will happen if I ask my
new mate to the sleepover?'; or 'What
is upsetting my friend?'.

Here are the meanings of the four suits and
then a detailed breakdown of what each card
means to a fortune teller.

◆ *Diamonds* are about all the day-to-day things
in life, good times, being with your friends,
parties, money, enjoyment and having fun.

♥ *Hearts* are about your feelings, your close
friends, the lads you like, your home life,
happiness and artistic abilities.

♣ *Clubs* are about ambitions, travel, getting
organized, expressing yourself, your thoughts
about your future and getting ahead in life.

♠ *Spades* are about new ideas, words,
discussions, school stuff, working,
meeting challenges, sometimes worries
and disagreements and getting your act
together to deal with these.

Diamonds

Ace – the start of something fabulous.

Two – things may be too busy, it's
hard to juggle school and friends, or home
and friends.

Three – make the most of yourself and work hard.

Four – cash-worries (although you probably have
no real need).

Five – don't lose the plot! What do you really
value? Guard it!

Six – good news about money and you're feeling
rather generous.

Seven – you have talents so don't hang about
in the background or be a couch potato – use
it or lose it!

Eight – don't compare yourself to
anyone, be positive about who you are.

Nine – you can have most things you want from new gear to great times!

Ten – something ends successfully.

Jack – a busy time, lots of short journeys, interesting news. Can mean a blond or red-haired young person.

Queen – this represents a popular, lively woman or girl – a party animal, but she may keep her real feelings hidden. She may be fair, blonde or red-headed.

King – a popular man or older boy, fair-haired, life-and-soul-of-the-party, with a secret ambitious streak.

Hearts

Ace – love, new romance, start of a new relationship, creative success.

Two – coming to an agreement, making an arrangement, making up after a quarrel.

Three – time to party! Friendships are great.

Four – feeling bored, but things will soon look up.

Five – feeling sad? Get over it! Make room for better things.

Six – someone from the past comes back into your life.

Seven – happy, happy, happy – but the biggest smiles of all may come through what at first looks the least attractive.

Eight – a relationship of some sort is ending, but it's ok as it's obviously for the best. Now there's room for something better.

Nine – a wish comes true.

Ten – something you have been working on comes to a successful conclusion.

Jack – love is on its way! This card can stand for a best friend, boyfriend or someone who loves you. It can also mean a young person with light brown or fair hair.

Queen – a loving, cuddly sort of woman or girl, who loves taking care of people. She may be fair or light-brown haired.

King – a really gorgeous guy but he has an emotional side and can be moody.

Clubs

Ace – a really exciting time is coming up – make the most of it!

Two – your position is better than you think, but be cautious all the same.

Three – you've made a good start, so keep going.

14

Four – you can see you're getting somewhere so kick back and relax for a while.

Five – don't give up! You'll soon get through those little setbacks.

Six – your friends all rate what you've achieved, so give yourself a pat on the back.

Seven – hmm, shaky ground, but keep your cool and you'll be fine.

Eight – busy, busy, busy and lots of hard work to do.

Nine – take stock, don't take any risks, play a waiting game.

Ten – you've taken on too much so don't be afraid to off-load – there's a way round this!

Jack – a supportive friend or a very helpful discussion with someone. This card can mean a young person with brown hair.

15

Queen – an organized, practical and clever woman who knows about the good things in life.

King – a capable and reliable man, probably a family man with a good reputation.

Spades

Ace – a decision must be made.
All you can think of is one thing.

Two – you need to face your fears to move forward – things will look much better then.

Three – someone may hurt you or lie to you but this time must be gone through to get to the better times that are ahead.

Four – you've been working too hard, so chill!

Five – bit of a red face here! Cut your losses and move on.

Six – a new start. Your problems are behind you, so don't mope!

Seven – you're in a bit of a sticky situation, but as long as you are true to yourself and do what you think is right, all will be fine.

Eight – there seems to be trouble all round and all you want to do is hide! But things aren't really that bad, so tackle them one at a time.

Nine – stop worrying! You are making things seem worse than they are.

Ten – things seem bleak but hang on in there because the darkest hour always comes before the dawn.

Jack – careful who you trust; don't spill your secrets. This card can be a young person with very dark or black hair.

Queen – a woman who has had a hard life and so keeps herself to herself – but her feelings run deeper than you imagine. Sometimes this card means a woman or girl who is spiteful, a stirrer and/or jealous.

King – a successful man in authority, like a school teacher or policeman. He may not be a very warm-hearted person and could be resentful.

⋆⋆ FOUR-CARD SPREAD

This is a more complicated spread that you can use to expand your talents. First of all take out a Queen or a Jack to represent you – choose the one that you feel most comfortable with, based on the previous descriptions. (You may feel that the character descriptions are more important than the hair colour.)

Place your card (or 'significator') in front of you and shuffle the rest of the pack. Dealing the cards face down, place one card on the left, one above, one to the right and one below the significator. The card on the left means the past, the one on the top present conditions, the one on the right the near future and the one at the bottom possibilities.

Let us say you are worried about going to a new school, or the start of a new term and you want to get some idea of how things are going to work out. You deal your four cards and then turn them up one by one, starting with the one on the left. In this case it is the Three of Hearts – no surprise! You've been having a ball and that's coming to an end. Now turn up the top card – this shows the Two of Spades, telling you that right now you have to look the future in the eye and make something good happen. Now turn up the card to the right. It is the Queen of Clubs showing that a very organized and sensible female is coming into your life, and this could be a friend or, more likely, a teacher or friend's mother. Now turn up the bottom card – it is the Seven of Diamonds, giving you a hint that you must use what you have to the full and make sure you exploit every chance you get.

Queens and Kings indicate people and Jacks usually do so, too, although they can also mean the thoughts of other people, and/or what they do. So if you turn up one of these you have the choice to shuffle again and deal another card to go with the picture card, to give you more information. So, in our example spread, if you wanted to know more about the Queen of Clubs, or simply more about the immediate future, you could deal another card to keep her company. Let us say this is the Two of Hearts. This would probably mean that this is a person you'll be making an agreement with. Or if it were the Six of Hearts she is someone from your past, or with links to it. Or if you dealt the Eight of Clubs it means there is a time of hard work coming up, probably connected to her. Let us say you dealt the worst card in the pack – the Ten of Spades. Well, the good news is that the only way is up! A challenging time is coming up, but the great thing is that you'll be stronger for it, and in our example spread the Seven of

Diamonds promises better things and lots of opportunities.

What if you deal all Spades? Don't freak out! Maybe your fears are affecting the cards. Remember, nothing can take away your free will, so learn from the positive comments that apply to every card. And if you really do need more information then deal another card, as in the example with the Queen of Clubs. Let the cards show you the optimistic side and find your best way forward.

A good fortune teller also uses her common sense and good judgement to make decisions so make sure you use yours! Keep an open mind, have some fun and remember that YOU are the key to your future, not the cards.

CHAPTER TWO

Crystal gazing

Can you see the future with a crystal ball? Yes,
to some extent, depending how much talent you
have, or develop. People who have the ability can
see images in a crystal, and this skill can be learnt
by almost anyone who wants it. Actually it is
called 'scrying' and you can do it with several
objects, not just a crystal ball. Anything you use
for scrying is called a 'speculum'. What the
speculum is helping you do is get in contact
with all the knowledge in your subconscious.
Just like all other forms of fortune telling –
YOU are the key!

The art of scrying

Scrying simply means looking for and perceiving images or messages in a suitable vessel, your speculum. Here is a list of possible speculums:

✱ A simple bowl of water, perhaps with a coin at the bottom, to focus on. If this is your choice it is a good idea to pick a suitable bowl and keep to the same one. The bowl should preferably be a dark colour and it is nicer to use a natural substance such as pottery rather than plastic.

✱ A dark mirror – i.e. a mirror that is blackened so you can't see your reflection. Such mirrors can be bought in many New Age shops and they cost about £20.

✱ Almost anything with a surface that reflects. Many crystal balls are really glass balls rather than crystal ones, for a large crystal may be very expensive indeed. Glass can be just as effective, however, if you like using it. You can even scry in something as small as the

24

diamond on your Mum's engagement ring, but that's more limiting.

✳ Some people can scry with patterns, such as you find on curtains or wallpaper, finding they 'see' faces and shapes, but this can be more difficult.

Of course, it is much nicer to have a proper crystal ball – the old traditions aren't there for nothing! There is something magical about the shape of a sphere, because it is perfect, smooth and a similar shape to our planet. If you are lucky enough to be able to buy a crystal ball, or have one given to you, it will make your scrying more pleasurable. Crystals are things of beauty and magic, and they are great inspiration for psychic stuff.

✦✦ CHOOSING A CRYSTAL BALL

It is possible to find crystal balls of all sizes, made out of a variety of crystals such as amethyst and rose quartz, among others. Some are only about four centimetres in diameter and come with their own little stand. These cost about £20. Some can be very expensive indeed.

As with so many matters, your greatest help in choosing a scrying crystal is your intuition – together with practical things such as cost. Decide first what you have to spend and choose from what is available. There is a lot to be said for crystal that is fairly clear. However, if you really love amethyst, for example, you can get good results with that, as it is a wonderful stone for helping you to be calm, and get in the dreamy mood you need for scrying. A crystal does not have to be perfect for scrying. Many seers find that small marks help them to focus. Nor does your crystal have to be round – you can use other shapes if you wish.

Here is a list of crystals and their characteristics which you might like to use for your scrying:

★ **Agate** – mental matters, healing, protection, love

★ **Amber** – luck, healing, beauty, love, strength

☆ **Amethyst** – psychism, peace, dreams, healing, happiness

☆ **Aquamarine** – purity, peace, psychism

☆ **Beryl** – love, finding lost objects, psychism

☆ **Citrine** – psychism, anti-nightmare

☆ **Diamond** – inspiration, flashes of insight

☆ **Emerald** – knowledge of past and future, money, protection

☆ **Haematite** – answering questions, focus, perception, grounding

☆ **Labradorite** – psychic protection, path in life

☆ **Obsidian** – peace, protection, insight, grounding

☆ **Quartz crystal** – power, psychism, healing

☆ **Rose quartz** – opens the heart, helps you tune into people's feelings

★★ CHOOSING A DARK MIRROR

Dark mirrors are not as easy to get as crystal balls and they may be more expensive than a small crystal. You are unlikely to have a wide choice. The mirror may well be packaged up. Ask to look at it, touch its surface and make sure you feel good with it before you get out your purse!

★★ PREPARING AND STORING YOUR SPECULUM

As we have seen, you can scry in any reflective surface, of any size. However, if you have chosen something especially for scrying it needs to be cleansed and prepared, which also helps you to focus your mind.

Hold your crystal or mirror in the running water of a stream, imagining all impurities leaving it and seeing it filled with light. If you can't get to a stream, soak it in spring water or filtered water – just running it under the tap isn't quite the same! Don't use salt water for crystals as it can damage them. (You can also cleanse a special bowl and coin for scrying, if you wish to use the bowl-of-water method.) Affirm that the cleansing water is opening a channel in your speculum so it will give you glimpses into the Otherworld.

When you feel that your speculum is cleansed, dry it with a soft white cloth and store it in a black velvet pouch, or in its box, somewhere safe. If it is a crystal it may be best to place it on top of a soft cloth and let it dry naturally.

Before putting it away, have a little dedication ritual. Light a white candle and burn a joss stick of lavender or jasmine. Place your speculum in front of you and say the following:

Great Mother, I thank you for leading me to this vessel.
May it be a channel of love, light and inspiration for me.
I dedicate it to the powers of light,
And ask you to protect and guide me.
Blessed Be.

Hold the speculum and close your eyes,
pouring love and warmth into it. Leave it on
your windowsill while the Full Moon shines so
it soaks up some of the Moon's mysterious magic.

Always store it carefully, putting it away after
each use and only bringing it out when you are
ready to scry. From time to time it is a good idea
to re-cleanse and re-dedicate your speculum, in
case it has picked up anything negative.

How to scry

You have your speculum, it is cleansed and ready
for use – what do you actually do?

Scrying is about 'seeing' pictures in the
speculum. Before you scry, make sure you are
relaxed and contented. Have a bath
containing lavender, if you wish. Get
your speculum ready, carefully light a
candle and settle yourself comfortably,
holding your speculum, if you like, or
placing it on a firm surface in front of you. You
may like to see the flame reflected in the surface,

or you may prefer it to be dark. Burning a jasmine joss stick can help to open your psychic senses.

If you are using a bowl of water to scry, you may like to experiment first, using a silver coin dropped in the bottom or with just water. If you find that a coin does help you to see images, it is best to keep the same coin to re-use. This is the cheapest method, if you're on a budget, but you will still feel 'special' if you keep to the same bowl and coin.

It's a good idea to ask a question to get you started. Remember, in all you do 'Harm none' is the rule, so don't try to find out things you aren't supposed to! The sort of question you might ask could be: 'What will be the best thing for me to do at the weekend – see my Nan, go skating or go shopping?'; 'Is this a good time to ask Mum for a rise in my allowance?'; 'Is that lad really interested in me?'; 'Which friend will give me the best advice when I go to buy my new party outfit?'. Ask questions that are connected to your life and let the speculum bring your instincts to the fore.

Look deep into the speculum, focusing on a point far away, below the surface. Soon you will start to see pictures. These may be with your actual eyes, but are more likely to be pictures in your mind. You may also find you get impressions, feelings, even taste, hear or smell things – this is a great indication that your psychic senses are working on all levels. Take note of all you perceive but don't be too quick to decide what it means, because it takes lots of time and practice to make sense of this ancient art.

What if you experience absolutely nothing? That is quite common at first. Don't strain, and don't despair. Ten minutes is quite enough for a first try – you can always have another go on another day.

⋆⋆YOUR INTERPRETATIONS

Be very careful how you interpret what you see in your speculum. Remember that lots of images will come from your own mind and while that is the pathway to developing your intuition it does NOT mean you should take things literally, or frighten yourself. For instance, if you see a monster it just means you are working your way through your fantasies and fears, on your way to developing insight. It may also mean that you feel guilty and think that scrying is 'wrong' – or it may just be that last night you were watching a scary movie! In the same way, seeing something like a skull doesn't mean anything sinister – it is far more likely to mean ancient knowledge. If you really do feel uneasy, then it's better not to attempt any scrying for now. Scrying should be peaceful, pleasant and make you feel you are expanding your awareness. It should make you feel good!

✦✶ PSYCHIC SAFETY

If you find you have a talent for scrying and you are getting some useful images then you need to protect yourself. In fact it is a good idea to do this anyway.

You can make yourself psychically safe by going round your room several times with a lavender joss stick, telling all negative 'vibes' to go away and imagining the lavender smoke getting rid of them. Ask the Great Mother or whatever god or goddess is meaningful to you, to protect you. Then imagine a sphere of blue light surrounding you and your speculum, while you are scrying.

The stone labradorite is protective, and easily obtained in New Age shops. Placing some near you or having four labradorite tumblestones around you roughly at North, South, East and West is a good idea.

Don't scry for too long – twenty minutes is plenty. When you have finished scrying, mentally re-absorb the energies of your blue sphere back into your body, take a deep breath and pat yourself on your tummy and legs. Thank your goddess or god. Go round the room again with your joss stick, and put out your candle, if you have been using one. Put your speculum away, make notes about what you have seen and go and do something ordinary like making a cup of tea and having a snack.

This will help to bring you back to the real world.

Enjoy yourself and see what exciting things you can discover about the future. Don't worry if you find you can't really see anything in your speculum. You can always try again another day. You may also find that you are better at other methods of fortune telling and you might like to concentrate on these. As always keep your feet firmly on the ground and live your everyday life to the full. The future is yours to shape – so make sure you shine in it.

CHAPTER THREE

Your psychic touch

Did you know that you can pick up lots of hidden information, just by touching an object? Being psychic isn't just about 'seeing things' and sensing things in the air – it is also about plugging in to all the information stored within ordinary things. This is how it works.

 When we use an object, or wear it, it absorbs some of our own special 'vibration'. If we have it close to us a very great deal, it absorbs even more, and if our emotions are strong then this is magnified. Some objects 'hold' this information more readily than others; for instance jewellery is more likely to carry a strong 'vibe' than a plastic beaker – although you never know! It is as if there is a 'memory' deep within the molecules of things, so that events and feelings are stored there, as if on a film. Some people who have studied mysterious things have said that water, in particular, stores information and that is why many ghostly sightings and spirit happenings occur where it is damp, or where there is an underground stream. However, objects that aren't at all 'watery' do give off these impressions, too.

If you imagine someone wearing a wedding ring for many years, just think how much of that person's nature may have gone into the ring. If they had some specific hope, sorrow or joy that went with them through life, then the ring would absorb it. So a woman who was very tense and always on the go would transfer that feeling to her ring. After she died – or just took the ring off – someone sensitive might well pick up all this tension and not want to touch the ring, although they might not be very sure why. Someone who was always happy and smiling, on the other hand, might leave a ring filled with joy that you somehow couldn't help slipping on your finger with a grin!

Whatever the case, you can pick up impressions from many objects, and you can learn to expand and use your awareness, if you try.

Getting touchy-feely

You can practise psychometry (the skill of picking up messages from things you touch) at any time and anywhere, just by holding things and seeing how you feel. But that isn't really a good idea for three reasons. Firstly, by doing this in such a casual way you can leave yourself open to too many impressions and some of them might not be good for you – you could feel tired, drained and 'funny'. Secondly, you probably won't have any way of checking out what you have sensed. And thirdly, if you really want to develop this gift then you owe it to yourself to get in the right frame of mind, especially at first.

The best way to do psychometry is to get a few good friends together, maybe at a sleepover, so you can all help each other.

Prepare yourselves like you would for scrying –
have a bath or shower using lavender soap and
make sure you feel relaxed. Cleanse the room by

burning a lavender joss stick. Candlelight is
great for anything psychic, so tell your Mum
what you're doing and ask her if it's ok to
have candles in your room. It doesn't matter if
you and your crew are a bit giggly, because being
playful relaxes you and makes you more psychic.
However, it's important this doesn't go too far, so
no-one should be silly or over-excited.

It's a good idea if everyone
brings a few things for the others to
test out their skills on. If you use
things like rings, bracelets, postcards
and other small items, these can be

placed in envelopes. Make sure the stuff each
person brings has a 'history' that they know about
and doesn't belong to them – after all, you'll
know loads about your friends without touching
anything that's theirs!

Pass each envelope round your circle, letting
each person hold it for as long as they
like. Place it first in one palm, then the
other. Which is best? Which do you find

most sensitive? Many people find they get
best results with their left palm, because
the left side of the body is connected to
the right side of the brain, which is
the instinctual, 'psychic' side. (This is reversed
in left-handed people.) Run your fingertips
over the envelope too.

Note what you are feeling. Several things
may happen:

* you may get a tingling in your hand and arm.
  If this happens, just relax because it means the
  impressions are getting through

* the object may feel hot or cold

* you may start to feel an emotion, such as
  happiness, sadness or anger

* you may 'see pictures' with your mind's eye

* you may 'hear' things, like a tune – this may
  just come into your mind from 'somewhere'

* you could become aware of a taste
  in your mouth

* you could imagine that you smell something

✳ a part of your body may start to ache, feel
funny, or want to move.

None of these sensations should be extreme or
unpleasant. If they are, stop immediately and start
on the pizza instead! This may happen because
you are anxious about what you are doing, or
it could be that the object has some nasty
impression on it. Whatever the case, no harm
at all can come to you.

✳✳ WHAT TO DO WITH THE INFORMATION

When you are doing this in a group it is much
better not to say anything at first or you will
influence everyone else. Write down everything
you sense on a piece of paper and pass the
envelope quietly to the next person. When you
have all had a go, then open the envelope and
take it in turns to say what you sensed. Then the
person who brought the object can tell you all
who it belonged to and how right you were!

Don't reject anything you 'pick up' because you don't think it makes sense, and do talk through what you feel with the owner of the object. It may seem at first you were wrong but after thinking and examining, you may be right. Don't be surprised if what you sense is confused. Once when I held an object in a group of friends, I found I could see many beautiful scenes with my mind's eye – mountains and lakes, snowy landscapes, everything looking fresh, bright and free – and yet the tears were spilling down my cheeks and I felt bereft and very old. It turned out that the article I had been holding belonged to the mother of my friend. She had always longed to go to Austria and Switzerland, to see the mountainous country that seemed magical to her. But she never got there and never made her family understand what this meant to her. All the while her dreams and her feelings of loss and unhappiness were going into her ring, to last long after her death – while hopefully her spirit was now able to visit her mountains and lakes, and many other wonderful things besides!

When you are going over the information, give yourself marks out of ten for how well you think you did. Keep this safe, so that when you next have a go you can see whether or not you have improved.

7

What use can you make of psychometry, if you become skilled at it? It is like any of the psychic arts – it gives you a little bit of extra knowledge and opens your awareness. It can be

of practical use if you are buying second-hand things at a car boot sale or charity shop – some things won't feel right and you will know to steer clear of them. Being able to pick up impressions like this will also help you know about people. When you touch someone's hand you can get a good idea about them through this contact, especially if you haven't already picked up all you want by other types of intuition.

★★ PROTECTING YOURSELF

Psychometry isn't dangerous – it is much safer than riding your bike to the shops in busy traffic! However, all the psychic arts need to be approached with common sense and caution. Sometimes we can be frightened by them, even though we don't really think we should be, because of all the scary things we may have heard or been taught. Then fear breeds fear and we can lose our cool!

If you don't have friends you can trust, or who share your interest by all means have a go on your own. Your Mum will probably have some jewellery that belonged to older family members and you could try with that. It could be interesting talking to your Mum about the things you feel and sense – possibly the past will be speaking to you quite clearly. Or you might come up with something far-fetched that turns out to be true when you do a little family research!

Whether you practise alone or in a group it is a good idea to have a little 'closing down' ritual when you finish doing psychometry. This will have the effect of shutting off your psychic senses, and that is a good idea, because if you stay 'open' you could feel a bit spaced out and muddly for a while.

Just close your eyes and imagine that you are a beautiful flower and that your petals are closing up, folding in over one another until you have become a tight, bright bud. Now pat yourself all over and touch your palms to the floor. Eat and drink something, and go back to ordinary things, such as watching a DVD or even your English essay. Who knows – your psychometry session may have given you real inspiration!

CHAPTER FOUR

The dice are right!

Want to know the answer to a question, quickly and simply? Then do what people have done for centuries – ask the dice! Legend tells us that

Julius Caesar threw a die (strictly speaking, when there is only one it is called a 'die') to make a decision about whether to cross the Rubicon river and march on Rome to take it over and rule it. But dice were already ancient in the time of the Roman Empire for they have been found in very old burial sites all over the world. Using them to cheat seems to be just as old, for many of these dice were 'loaded' meaning they had been shaved on one side to affect the way they fell!

As with all forms of divination
(ways of fortelling the future and other

hidden matters) there are lots of rules, some of which contradict each other. Like all fortune telling, the point is to get in touch with your own instincts and the power of your intuition. In time you'll develop the best way to use the dice but for now, here are some handy guidelines.

✶✶ GETTING READY

You will need three dice, a container or bag to shake them in and/or store them, and a piece of cloth or paper over 30 cm square.

First you need to draw a clear circle, with chalk or pen, on the cloth or paper. This circle should be 30 cm in diameter. The easiest way to do this is to raid the kitchen for a nice big bowl to draw round.

The first time you do this you may be happy using the old dice from your Snakes and Ladders box, but if you decide you are going to be a real Dice Diviner, then you might like to choose some that feel really special, in a colour, or colours that you like. Some people feel better results come with natural materials so go for wood, or even bone, if possible, rather than plastic. Store your dice in a black velvet bag and never use them for anything other than divining. You can use the bag for shaking, or a cup. If you're serious about this you'll want a special cup that you keep for this alone. A good choice might be an earthenware or china mug with your Zodiac Sign on it. Go with what feels good to you.

★ ★ STARTING OUT

Of course you can just mess about with the dice, asking daft questions and having a chuckle, and that's fine. But if you want proper results, it's best to be a bit more serious. Make sure you're in a nice, relaxed state of mind before you throw, and maybe heat some oil of lavender in an oil burner, to clear your head. It's a great idea to involve one or two special friends – in fact some traditions say that someone else should always throw the dice for you, when you ask the question.

Ready to throw? Make sure your circle is spread out, nice and flat. The dice should be thrown about 30 cm above the circle. Think about your question until you can express it clearly and simply. For instance, 'Will I do well in Maths?' is a better question than 'Which subject should I concentrate on when revising?'. For some questions you may need to throw more than once, if the answer isn't clear.

1 2 3
4 5 6
7 8 9

There's no harm in being a bit giggly, but everyone should be silent before the throw, and you should just ask the question inside your head – you can tell your friends what it was after you get the answer, if you like. But remember, no-one has to spill the beans if they don't want to. All true seers and fortune tellers know when to keep their mouths shut!

Reading the dice

Wise people tell us that the dice speak of the future, never the present or the past, and that what they foretell takes place within nine days. Your three dice will fall, each with a side uppermost, and it is the number of spots on that side that you count. You add up the total of the three and the answer to your question is given by the total number of spots.

You should only count the spots on the dice that fall inside the circle. If they all fall outside, pick them up and try again. If they all fall outside a second time, pack them away until another day, because they're telling you this isn't a good time for a reading. Here are the meanings:

One

You can only get this if two of the dice have fallen outside the circle. It means 'Yes' loud and clear to what you've asked about. If your question doesn't involve yes or no, this is just a very positive result – the dice are saying 'Go for it!'. For instance, you might have asked: 'What will happen if I go to Amy's party?' and this result tells you you'll have a ball! Of course you could have kept it really simple and asked: 'Should I go to Amy's party?' – but if she's a good friend you would probably be going anyway!

 ## Two

Sorry, but this one is a big 'No'. A thumbs down to whatever your question was. Disappointing? Only for a while – better things are just around the corner.

Three

Great! Pleasant surprises are on their way and there could be some good news that you didn't expect, arriving out of the blue.

 ## Four

Hmm – not so good. There are difficulties ahead and you may get some unwelcome news, but if

you stay practical and sensible you can
turn it to the good. For instance you might
have asked if that gorgeous lad rates you
and if you throw a four it means that there
are problems. This doesn't mean there's no hope –
maybe he lives too far away or is too busy with
his mates and footie. As long as you don't stress
there's still hope for the future – and in any case
there might be another lad coming along ...

Five

Someone new is coming into your life and this
will be happy and exciting. No point trying to
work out who because this will probably be the
very last person you would have thought of!

Six

Watch out! You are liable to lose something.
Look after your purse and anything you
value. Look after your friends, too, and
anything you have achieved, such as being
captain of the netball team. No-one and nothing
can take from you what is rightfully yours, but

53

this number warns you not to take it for granted. The thing you need to look after will probably be in relation to the question; for instance if it was about schoolwork, then don't lose your books and pencil case!

Seven

Careful who you confide in, because someone could have a big mouth and your secrets could be all over school! If your question was about money, this isn't a good time to barter sweets on the school bus or to take a new paper round – but things could well be different next week.

Eight

If you go ahead with whatever you're asking about, people will run you down. They may blame you for anything that goes wrong, even if it's someone else's fault. Think carefully about your decision, but if it really feels right for you, then who cares? Go for it!

Nine

You and that lad are soon going to be getting together! Or you and your friend, or your Mum, brother or sister, are going to be getting along really well. If you've had a quarrel with someone, Nine gives you the opportunity to kiss and make up. If this seems to be nothing to do with your question, you may soon see how a close relationship helps it along.

Ten

Now is the start of something new and special. This might be a fresh project or activity, from decorating your room to taking up a new sport. If money is involved that will go well too.

Eleven

Someone or something is going out of your life. But don't stress – this is only for a while.

Twelve

Watch your mobile for a text bringing good news. This could come by email or letter, too.

Thirteen

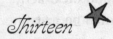

This spooky number is not good news at first. It means there will be challenges and things might not go your way. Only go ahead with your decision if you are really determined. Be prepared for some not-so-good surprises. You might get upset, but you can win through if you are sure this is right for you. Thirteen is a number that rewards people who have faith in themselves and who are willing to turn 'bad luck' into good.

Fourteen

A new friend is coming into your life and you'll be so glad you met. This person will be a great help to you and your friendship is likely to last a very long time.

Fifteen

No copying your friend's work or forging a sick
note to get off swimming! Fifteen warns you that
you'll get caught and things will be worse for you.
Always follow your conscience and do exactly
what you feel is right – then you'll be just fine.

Sixteen

A happy journey is coming up,
although it might be a complete
surprise. It is likely to be mega-important and
could be a turning point in your life.

Seventeen

Keep an open mind. A letter or email from abroad
could mean you have to change your plans.

Eighteen

The highest number of all tells you that
your wishes will come true and any question you
have asked has a favourable answer. Happiness
and success are on their way – lucky you!

✶✶ LET'S LOOK AT SOME EXAMPLES

It only takes a little imagination to link the answers the dice give to any question you may ask. However, some are not as straightforward as others. Here are some that might make you think ...

Q. Does that gorgeous lad rate me?

A. 17 So what could that mean? Maybe the dice are telling you your question is not important and that better things (and even more gorgeous lads!) will soon be on your mind. It could also mean that you find out something that turns you off the lad, that you shouldn't concentrate too much on one boy, or that you are going to go on holiday soon and forget him. Basically, other things are important now – but he might come up again later!

Q. Is my best friend to be trusted?

A. 11 It would be easy to interpret this as you and your friend splitting up. But it could equally mean the mistrust leaving your life. Whenever there is doubt, keep your head. If you assume the worst, you could create it!

Q. Should I go horse riding or have ballet classes? (Assuming your folks won't pay for both.)

A. 10 Well, you didn't ask a simple question – it would have been better to ask 'Should I go horse riding?' and throw again for ballet if you thought the answer was 'No'. However, Ten seems to be telling you that it'll be the start of something great, whatever you do!

Q. How can I get more money?

A. 9 So how can making it up with someone or getting close to them affect your purse situation? Maybe the next nine days will show you how! It could mean that your parents realize what an angel you are and give you a raise. Alternatively, the dice could be telling you that money isn't the most important thing right now and that you will soon realize it.

Q. How can I be more popular at school?

A. 4 Not the answer you might have wanted (but your question wasn't very well put!). Four is indicating that you'll have to put in some hard work and practical effort, and that it may take a while. Maybe you could join a club? Ask the dice again to help you decide, and keep your questions to the point.

THE DICE IN THEIR PLACE

You can have great fun with the dice and sometimes they can give you some helpful pointers. But always remember that they do not have all the answers! If you feel something very strongly in your heart, then that is the way for

you. Of course, it is important that
you can tell the difference between
being stubborn and silly, and really
being in contact with your intuition,
but if you think about it you will know.

   If you have to make up your mind about
something really significant, or if you are worried
about something, then don't use the dice because
your worries and tension will get in the way and
you won't get a good reading. It is much better
in a case like that to talk things over with an
adult you can trust and use your common sense.

   As with all types of divination, look on the
dice as if they are a wise and helpful friend,
who usually has good advice, sometimes teases
you and sometimes gets it wrong. Keep a light
heart and a light touch – and the dice will fall
your way.

CHAPTER FIVE

Clever cuppa

One old-fashioned way to take a peek into the future is by reading tea leaves. These days we mostly use tea bags, but real tea is easy enough to get in supermarkets or health-food stores, and if you use that you will feel just like the old village wise-woman from long ago! There is something magical about 'brewing up' your fortune-telling potion, rather like Paige in *Charmed*. You don't have to drink it for it to work!

Reading tea leaves is actually called 'tasseomancy' and it began in China many centuries ago. It became popular in Europe in the eighteenth century, when tea was a luxury, and very expensive. Getting started on reading tea leaves these days won't cost you more than a magazine if you shop carefully, and once you've got the gear it's free – until you run out of tea!

⋆⋆ GETTING READY

You can use the stuff in your Mum's kitchen, if she doesn't mind, but it is more fun to get your own tasseomancy kit, and then you can keep it specially for your potions. You will need a teapot that lets plenty of leaves flow into the spout, so look carefully in the charity shops until you find one you think will be ok. You will also need a cup and saucer. Choose a cup that is white inside, with a good handle that you can grab hold of, and smooth sides, because the leaves will stick to any ridges. A wide, bowl-shaped cup will make it easier for you to swill the tea round – you'll see why this is important later. If you want to make the most of this you can choose a pot and cup and saucers that are really lovely – it's up to you. It is best to have at least two suitable cups, so you can share your tasseomancy with a friend.

You will also need some tea, of course. Go for some good quality tea, with large leaves. You may need to experiment with one or two brands. Japanese tea is not suitable because the leaves are too long. Chinese tea is usually better than Indian tea, and one sort that tends to work well is Keemun tea.

If you like you can read coffee grounds. Make the coffee in a pot, not a cafetiere. It might take several tries to find a coffee that gives good results. Whether you're using tea or coffee, you don't want to use a strainer – you want plenty left in your cup for your psychic powers to work on!

Reading the leaves

As with any form of fortune telling, traditions have grown up that tell you exactly how to go about it. You don't have to follow them, but there is something about a tradition, especially when doing anything magical, that helps you to 'plug in' to ancient wisdom and all the powers of your intuition. Here is the method, starting from the very basics, in case you've never made a proper cuppa before!

Fill the kettle with water, enough to fill your teapot. When the kettle boils, pour a little water in, to 'warm the pot'. Swill this round and pour it away. Now put in your tea. The old way of doing this was to use one heaped teaspoon per cup and 'one for the pot'. If you have a large pot and are going to read (and drink!) several cups then you will need to brew up four or five teaspoons of tea, but if you only have a one-cup pot, then one or two will do.

When your tea leaves are in your warmed pot, pour the boiling water on and stir clockwise with a teaspoon. You could now say:

★ *Blessed tea leaf, warming brew*
Show me the future, clear and true
Blessed Be.

Wait a few minutes for the tea to 'brew' – unless you want it very weak. Pour some milk in each of the cups to be used and pour in your tea, adding sugar to taste if you wish. The real tradition states that the reading should be taken from the first cup poured, but if you and some friends are doing it together you won't want to keep brewing up a new pot, so there is no harm in reading several cups together.

Be mentally calm and relaxed as you sip your tea. If you hate tea, then you can pour it carefully down the sink, but whether you drink it or chuck it you should leave a teaspoonful of liquid in the bottom of the cup. Concentrate on what you are doing – you can repeat the little rhyme just given if you like. If you have a question to ask, word it clearly in your mind.

Each person having a 'reading' needs to have their own cup, and what is seen in that cup refers to them alone. Hold the cup in your right hand, by the handle. Now swill the liquid round the cup three times, in an anti-clockwise direction. If you are left-handed you can hold the cup in your left hand, of course, but still make sure the liquid goes anti-clockwise. If you live in the southern hemisphere, however, it is a good idea to go clockwise instead. When you have swilled round, move the cup

to your other hand and quickly turn it upside-
down on the saucer. Wait a few moments to make
sure all the liquid has drained out and the tea
leaves or coffee grounds are settled in place. Then
turn the cup back over. You are ready to read!

✶ ✶ SEEING THE FUTURE

The shapes formed by the tea leaves in the cup
are what will give you a clue about what is going
to happen, but where they are placed is very
important too. Shapes near the rim of the cup are
about what is happening now, or just about to
happen. The middle of the cup is about the future
and the bottom of the cup is the distant future.
What does this mean? Well, the top of the cup
represents days; the middle, weeks; and the
bottom months or even years in the future.
The place where the handle joins the cup is
the part that links directly with the person
having the reading.

In the cup the leaves or grounds will form
shapes – you just need your imagination to see

them and your intuition
to decide what they mean.
Just look into the cup in a
relaxed and dreamy way. It can help if you let
your eyes go out of focus, so the tea leaf shapes
go all blurred – then you may find pictures start
to appear. Often your first thought will be your
best thought – don't be afraid of sounding
stupid! Usually there will be more than one
shape in the cup, so start with the biggest and
go from there.

✱ ✦ SHAPING UP!

Often the things you see will be symbols, not
things you take to be exact. For instance, if you
see a flower that probably doesn't mean anything
to do with the garden, or even that someone is
going to give you a bunch of them! Think about
 what a flower represents. It means beauty – so
if your question had been 'Does that cute lad
rate me?' a flower in your cup is a big 'Yes –
he thinks you're gorgeous!'. If it had been 'Is

the weather going to be nice tomorrow?'
then a flower is more difficult to
interpret and you would have to ask
yourself if, in your own mind, you link
flowers with sunshine or rain.

As you practise, reading the leaves will become
easier. Keep your questions very simple at first,
just about things that are going to happen over

 the next few days. Make a note of what
shapes you get and how you interpret
them, and match these up with what
actually happens. Often it turns out that
one of the gang is really good with tea leaves,
someone else is great with the dice and another
person is brilliant at psychometry. It just depends
what you're drawn to and what you feel at home
with. Here is a list of some of the shapes you
might see and what they may mean.

 Acorn – oak trees grow from these, so an acorn
is a sign of a big idea getting started. It is
a sign of fertility so it could also mean
someone getting pregnant!

Aeroplane – a holiday, a long journey. If the point
of the aeroplane is pointing downwards there

could be a disappointment, but you'll find a way through it.

Anchor – something is holding you back (especially lower in the cup) or this could mean a trip over the water or news connected with boats.

Angel – you are being watched over and cared for.

Ball – this means something is getting 'rolling' for you. But if lots of things are looking stressful, best keep your head down for a while!

Balloon – any troubles will soon blow away. Or someone is going to have a party. Have you forgotten anyone's birthday?

Bed – you need to kick back and relax (or possibly it's time for a sleepover!).

Bee – you'll be busy, busy, busy.

Bell – surprising news.

Bird – good news is coming. Or someone is going to buy you a budgie – or maybe you need to feed the birds in your garden.

Bold – you're doing really well at school, it's a good time to study, especially if the book is open. A closed book can mean secrets.

Broom – sort out your bedroom, you might find something!

 Candle – you're just going to have to wait for a while …

Car – short journeys, longer journeys, things getting moving and getting going. If you had asked a question such as 'Is Dad going to take us to the cinema?' then a car would probably mean 'Yes'!

Cat – this can mean a variety of things from good luck through comfort and relaxation to catty comments – or it could mean a new kitten in the family! It all depends what the cat looks like.

Clouds – a few problems on the horizon, but they'll soon pass.

Crown – success! Or you get picked to play the Queen in the school play!

Cup – happiness, especially emotional. Or should you think about making Mum a cuppa, for once?

Dog – a good friend. Help may be needed. A new puppy may be on the way.

Ear – listen carefully, you don't want to miss anything.

Egg-timer – don't delay doing important things. Get your homework in on time, answer messages etc.

Eye – keep your eyes open, something isn't as it seems.

Face – if the face is smiling this means happiness and/or a kind person. If it's a miserable face then there is someone around that you're better off keeping away from. More than one face means a party. If you had asked a question like 'Did someone take my maths homework or did I just lose it?' a face would give you the hint that someone had nicked it!

Flowers – celebration, gifts, a wedding.

Fruit – mega good luck!

Guitar – if you had asked about guitar lessons then you are being advised to take them. But a guitar could also mean dancing, a celebration, a holiday to Spain or a lad who plays the guitar.

Gun – this could mean arguments and lots of squabbles, so get ready to button it for a while.

Heart – love and affection – what else?!

Horseshoe – lucky, lucky you!

Key – you are going to find the answer to something.

Knife – watch your temper! Look out for accidents with sharp objects, too.

Letters of the alphabet – these are usually the
initials of a person or place that's important
to you.

Moon – you will need to use your inner wisdom
soon, as you could be deceived or deceive
yourself. You should also take
note of your dreams. A crescent
moon that looks like your right
hand held up and cupped can mean the start
of a new cycle in your life; if it points the
other way, something is moving out of your
life (these meanings are best reversed in the
southern hemisphere).

Numbers – these often refer to days, weeks or
months depending where they are in the cup.
If you have asked a question that can be
answered in numbers, such as 'How much will
Mum raise my allowance?' then there you
have it (hopefully pounds, not pennies!).
Numbers could also be part of a telephone
number, a house number or a birthday.

Phone or mobile – a message is coming.
Should you be texting someone?

Purse – money! This could mean a raise in your allowance. It could also mean that you'll be given something valuable.

Question mark – this is a time when you just can't be sure. It may be best to read the leaves again a few days later. Are there any other symbols that make things clearer?

Ring – this means some sort of partnership. The most likely one is an engagement or marriage, but it could be a deep friendship. If you have asked a question about whether someone really wants to be with you or whether a friendship will last then a ring says 'Yes'.

Snail – don't rush, especially into a decision.

Square – things are going to go on in the same way. You can rely on what you want, but you might get bored.

Star – your wish will come true! ★

Sun – happiness. This could also mean the success of a creative project, such as customizing your jeans. It could also mean great weather for an outing.

Train – this has similar meanings to 'car'.

T-shirt or dress – new clothes, a special date or a big hint to sort out your room! Which do you think?

Umbrella – watch out! There's a spot of trouble on its way that you'll have to sort out (or maybe it's just going to rain and rain ...).

It is impossible to cover every shape you may see, or to give every meaning that a shape might carry – the ones listed here are just hints.

Always remember that your instincts count, so develop them. Play with ideas and have a chuckle at what you see. The tea leaves aren't there to tell you anything bad – just to give you a nudge in the right direction, so take everything for the positive pointer that it is – and drink up!

CHAPTER SIX

Casting the stones

Up until this part of the book all the methods of fortune telling we've looked at have meant using ordinary stuff that you can find round the house, for the most part. It's time now for us to look at a way of telling the future that will involve a little more work for you. If you choose to do this it will mean this 'method' becomes quite personal to you and gives you the opportunity to develop as a true 'seer'.

The old name for this method is 'lithomancy' and it can be very simple – although as you progress you may find you make more and more complex readings. It involves casting stones on to a cloth and interpreting the way they fall. Each of the stones has a special meaning. Here are some guidelines, although you are free to make your own variations if you like and even to add extra stones for specific reasons.

⋆⋆ GETTING THE GEAR

Firstly, and most importantly, you will need thirteen stones. You can buy tumblestones for about £1 each, in many New Age shops, and you can choose to use these, or you can collect your own pebbles – or you can use a mixture of the two. Just make sure that all the stones are a similar size, about the size of marbles. Here is a list of what you will need the stones for and suggestions for the semi-precious tumblestones that you could get.

1. SUCCESS – carnelian or amber (orange/gold stone).

2. SPORT AND ENERGY (things like running, walking, blading, skating) – garnet (red stone).

3. HOME – moss agate or a stone with green markings. Moonstone is also a possibility, and this is milky-white. Either types of colouring go with 'home'.

4. SPOOKY – apache tear (a dark stone with white markings) or any dark stone.

5. LADS – rhodochrosite – this is a raspberry pink stone which can represent strong feelings. Any reddish stone could do, but don't get mixed up with the 'sport and energy' stone!

6. MATES – rose quartz, this is a very pretty pale pink stone. It also relates to love but because it is 'affectionate' it is also good for friendships.

7. MONEY – jade, or any rich green stone.

8. NEWS – agate or citrine. (There are many types of agate so choose one that looks lively and varied such as a banded red-orange agate.)

9. PROBLEMS/CHALLENGES/HITCHES/
HARD WORK – onyx or any black stone.

10. GOOD LUCK – amethyst (or another
purple stone).

11. MUSIC/DANCE and PARTYING – lapis
lazuli, or a pretty blue stone.

12. JOURNEYS – tourmalated
quartz (this is a white
crystal shot through with
black markings). Or you can

choose any stone which looks 'busy'. Just
be careful it is easy to distinguish from
your 'news' stone.

13. YOUR STONE – finally choose a stone to
stand for you, when you do your 'throw'.
You can choose any stone that appeals.
You can duplicate one of the above stones,
if you really like it, but make sure you can
tell the difference! Ideally you should
choose a different stone, so if amethyst is
your favourite and you really want it to

represent you, find another purple stone
such as fluorite for your 'luck bringer'.

If you are pairing up with a friend
to do this, she could also have her
own special stone and you could
do throws together.

If you want to collect all or some of your
stones, go for a leisurely walk in the country –
or, better still, on a beach, and just see what you
can find. Sometimes you will find really special
stones such as ones with naturally occurring holes
all the way through – called 'holey stones' and

 these are very lucky. So are small fossils or
stones with crosses or stars on them. It is
best not to be in too much of a hurry if
you want to do this method – the more care you
take, the more relaxed you are and the more
personal your selection of stones, the better the
basis will be for your fortune telling.

★ ★ CLEANSING YOUR STONES

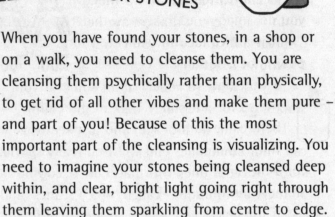

When you have found your stones, in a shop or on a walk, you need to cleanse them. You are cleansing them psychically rather than physically, to get rid of all other vibes and make them pure – and part of you! Because of this the most important part of the cleansing is visualizing. You need to imagine your stones being cleansed deep within, and clear, bright light going right through them leaving them sparkling from centre to edge.

If you can get to a clear, running stream, hold the stones in the glistening water, one by one, and imagine them being totally purified. Do this with each one individually until you feel sure it is clean, and then do it for a minute or two longer. If you can't get to a stream, just soak the stones in spring water – water from a bottle will do. Don't use salt water as this can change the structure of some stones. Let the stones dry naturally on a white towel – don't rub at them. You could also cleanse your stones by passing them through the vapour of a lavender joss stick, or by burying them overnight in organic wholemeal rice (throw the rice away afterwards – don't eat it!). Whatever you do, imagine each stone wonderfully cleansed.

It is a nice idea to dedicate your stones to the powers of Good in the Universe and to do this simply light a white candle and carefully lay the stones around it, on a white cloth. Sit before the candle with your hands on your thighs palms upwards, close your eyes and ask for a blessing. Imagine light flowing down and shimmering on your stones.

If possible leave your stones out in the light of the Full Moon for a night, to get them 'charged up'. Now they are ready to use.

⋆⋆ STORING YOUR STONES

Keep your stones in a special soft drawstring bag. You could make this, if you're feeling creative, using a circle of felt with holes punched in it, and a piece of cord which you thread through, or you could sew a little pouch – it's up to you. It is easy to buy little bags in New Age shops and they don't cost much. Choose something you like and feel comfortable with, which will easily contain all your stones. You may find it more convenient to have a bag that is big enough for you to put your hand in and take out the stones in a handful.

You will also need a square of soft fabric such as fake fur, felt, fleece or anything similar. This should be black, and about a metre square. You will also need a piece of cord, about three metres long, to form a circle on the square of fabric. The best colour for the cord is red, although any colour that appeals will do. Now you have all you need to start. Make sure you keep all your gear somewhere safe, only handle it when you want to tell your fortune and put it away afterwards. Only let a friend use your stones if you feel quite happy about this, and cleanse your stones again afterwards (unless you've decided to share your stones). If you have a really big falling out with a stone-sharing friend then it is best to bury the stones and start again with your own set. You could also use one set with a gang of mates, each having your own 'personal' stone. If someone leaves the gang in a friendly way, maybe because their folks move away, let them take their stone, or bury it. If there is any falling out, however, it may be best to start again, or at least thoroughly cleanse the stones. However, with any luck the stones will form a bond and you'll all get on better with this psychic link!

THROWING THE STONES

It is a good idea to make a little 'ritual' of throwing your stones because then you will be in the right mood and it will make the whole thing more magical. Light a candle and burn a joss stick – jasmine is a good perfume to choose. Set out your square of cloth and your circle of cord, ready to receive the stones. Compose your question clearly in your mind. Close your eyes for a moment, empty your mind and ask to be blessed.

Now take out the stones and warm them between your palms before throwing them. You can throw them all at once if you like, if you can hold them within your cupped palms. Or you can throw them in several bunches. Try to throw them in a casual way – do not try to affect how they fall, but be gentle with them so they do not chip. Say:

> *By stones of wisdom, stones enchanted*
> *My wish for second sight be granted.*

3 Tradition tells us that you can cast the stones three times at one sitting. After that, pack them up and wait for another day.

Interpreting the stones

This is the bit where you are going to need plenty of practice before you feel really confident that you can interpret the stones. It just isn't possible to go through all the different ways the stones might fall, and all the questions you might like to ask. It can be a very good idea to have a friend with you, who is really into this sort of thing, because she may be able to be more detached about your questions – and you will be the same about hers. Also, two heads are better than one!

Keep a notebook by you when casting the stones, make a note of how they fall, and how you interpreted them. Leave a space to write down, preferably in a different colour, what actually happened. After you have done this a few times you will begin to see how things are working out and find you can interpret the stones more easily.

The simplest question, which IS easy to interpret, is a Yes/No one and for this all you need are three stones – your personal stone, your black stone and your purple stone (that is your 'problems' stone and your 'luck' stone). The answer comes with the stone that falls closest to your personal stone. If it is the 'problems' stone, then the answer is 'No'. If the 'luck' stone is closest then it is 'Yes'. If the stones are about the same distance then this could mean the question is not as important as you think, or that the answer is not certain, or complicated in some way. Or it could just mean this is the wrong time to ask and the Cosmos isn't going to give away any secrets right now.

For more complicated throws, take the left-hand side of the circle to mean the past, the right-hand side to mean the future, the top of the circle to mean what is obvious and the bottom to mean what is hidden. Naturally some parts of the circle will be on the borderline, like some parts of life.

However, for some throws you may not feel that you need to take the parts of the circle into account – you may be able to interpret just by looking at how close the stones are to your special stone. In many throws a great number of the stones might not seem that important, especially if they are a long way away from your personal stone. Remember it is the stones that fall closest to your personal stone that hold the key to your question. The further away a stone falls the less it has to do with the matter in hand.

Let's look at some example questions ...

What sort of a friend is this new girl that I've started to hang out with?

Maybe you like this girl but you aren't quite sure whether you can trust her. If the stones fall with the rose quartz stone right next to yours then she's solid gold! If the 'lad' stone falls in between, then she could like the same boy as you and compete with you, especially if the 'problems' stone falls close by. If the rose quartz stone falls miles away from your stone then you probably won't have much in common and any stone that falls between can be telling you about the things that are likely to get in the way. BUT – and this is where skill and practice come in – the stones that lie between could be telling you about things that will bring you together, depending what they are and how close they are. For instance, your stone might fall a bit to the left of the circle and slightly low down. This could mean you are 'stuck' in the past and you have hidden feelings, maybe jealousy, maybe remembering you've been let down before and expecting it to

happen again etc. On the right may be the blue
stone, for partying and dancing, or the red 'sport'
stone, or the 'news' stone – or all of them! – and
then the rose quartz stone, which stands for your
friend. This could mean that you are going to get
closer to that girl because you are both going to
get an invitation to a swimming party, you are
going to have fun together etc. Even if the 'lad'
stone falls between you it is possible a boy could
bring you together – for instance you
might get a crush on her brother!

How will I do in my test?

Well, if your stone comes near the top of the
circle that's a good sign, and if it has the 'luck'
or 'success' stone close by it looks like you'll be
top of the class! If the 'mate' stone comes close
then friends will be important. Will they help or
hinder you? Look for the black 'problems' stone
for a hint, and if it is close then be prepared to
tell the gang to butt out while you study. If the

'home' stone is near yours then it is best to
work hard at home. If the blue stone falls
close to your stone together with the

'problems' stone then too much partying can be your downfall. If your stone falls near the bottom of the circle very close to the black, 'problem' stone, please don't panic! Remember, the stones are giving you a glimpse of what COULD happen. They don't seal your fate. Part of the reason for using fortune telling is because 'forewarned is forearmed' and if you know something may be on its way you can take steps to change things.

Does that lad rate me?

Chances are that's the kind of question that you'll be asking over and over again! Of course, this can be often answered by a simple Yes/No throw. But using all the stones will provide you with a more complete answer – and give you a hint about what to do to get his attention. So, if your stone and the 'lad' stone fall closest together, need we say more? If the 'problems' stone falls close to yours, especially if it falls between you and the 'lad' stone then there will be lots of obstacles to overcome. Of course, this doesn't mean he doesn't rate you necessarily, but it is likely, for whatever reason, that going after him will be more trouble than it's worth, so it is best to concentrate on someone else. If the blue stone falls near either of you, or between you, then you could get together at a party or disco, or if it's the red stone then sport could be what brings you together. The 'success' or 'luck' stone between you or close to either is a good sign. The 'news' stone close by means a text or message about him, or from him. Generally the stones closest to you will tell you what is influencing you and the stones between you and the 'lad' stone are the ones to pay most attention to.

What sort of a holiday will I have?

Here is a nice, general question that lets the stones speak! Look first for your own stone. If it's at the top of the circle you'll probably be out and about strutting your stuff, while if it's at the bottom you are more likely to be curled up with a book most of the time. If your stone is to the left then you'll probably be doing things you've done before, maybe going back to old places; if to the right then some new adventures are in store. If the 'journeys' stone is close to you then travel is

likely, or lots of short trips. If the 'spooky' stone is there then maybe the hotel will be haunted (or you and your friends will spend a lot of time with this book!). If the 'lad' stone is close then holiday romance is coming, and if the 'money' stone is there, look forward to lots of retail therapy (or working hard washing cars to make some money – groan!). If the black stone comes close, don't despair and decide to hide all summer under the duvet! Just watch out that your folks check passports, tickets and bookings and make sure you've got

plenty of books in your hand-luggage to read at the airport if the plane is delayed.

 What's the best way to celebrate my birthday?

The big day's coming up, your friends all want you to do different things and your Mum's leaving it up to you. Nightmare! But what would work out best? If your stone falls in the top part of the circle it's best to go out; if to the bottom, it looks like a sleepover; if to the left then do something tried-and-tested; if to the right try something new. Now look at the other stones – the blue one lying close means party time, the red one means something active, the 'lad' stone means invite some boys, the 'journeys' stone means take a trip (maybe to a theme park?). The green stone may mean hit the High Street to buy some new clothes, the 'news' stone may mean a letter or text will make up your mind for you. The 'success' and 'luck' stones mean you can't go wrong anyway, the 'problems' stone says make sure you plan things properly and maybe this won't be the best birthday ever (but it doesn't mean a disaster!).

How can I make more friends?

Not feeling as popular as you'd like to be? Don't worry – everyone feels that way at times. Throw the stones for this question to get some hints – red stone, do more sport, anything at all that appeals even a bit. Blue stone it's dancing;

'home' stone then invite them to yours; 'lad' stone could mean you're just too hot, so give the gang some flirting tips so they don't think you're stealing the show. The 'money' stone could mean you need to be more generous. Of course, you should never feel you have to 'buy' friends, but it does help if you are prepared to swap lip gloss and hair slides. The 'spooky' stone hints at telepathy games or sharing your *Amazing You* books. Obviously the 'luck' and 'success' stones give you the message that things are going to work out fine for you. The 'problems' stone tells you that you need to do some solid spadework – maybe you need to talk openly to your best friend about what you may be doing that makes people hesitate to get close to you. Maybe you've got a talent for putting your foot in it, for instance – you can change! The same sort of interpretations can be used for 'How can I get the lads to like me?' with slight changes. For instance the green 'money' stone could be a hint to buy more fantastic outfits – use your imagination!

★ ★ ★ ★ ✳ ★ ★ ★

Once you have a 'feel' for your stones you may want to extend the meanings. For instance you may find that the 'success' stone is giving you a hint to push yourself into the spotlight, or that the 'problems' stone is asking you to stop and think. This stone is sometimes about a teacher, authority figure or schoolwork, and that it isn't necessarily about anything unpleasant. The 'home' stone may often say a lot about your Mum or Dad; the 'news' or 'journeys' stones may also mean a visitor, a change, a surprise or a new way of looking at things; the 'money' stone can mean all possessions and the 'sport' stone also refers to health. All the meanings can be extended and become more complicated and meaningful as you 'flesh them out' with experience.

Always back up your stone throwing with common sense and good judgement. Don't just rely on the stones – they can give you useful pointers about aspects of your life but they don't tell the whole story. Use the stones to strengthen your intuition and you'll be amazed at the results. Happy throwing – and may the stones always roll your way!

CHAPTER SEVEN

Mother Nature knows

There are many old ways of telling the future from natural happenings in the world around us. Birds were considered especially magical creatures because they are able to fly through the air, and people used to believe they were messengers of the gods. Today we know better, of course. However, as with all things it is your mind that makes the link, your mind that interprets what you see, and so if the way birds are behaving gives you a 'feeling' then maybe it is important for you.

✦✦ MAGPIES

There is a well-known rhyme about seeing magpies that you may already have heard. Here is one version:

One for sorrow, two for joy
Three for a girl, four for a boy,
Five for silver, six for gold,
Seven for a secret, never to be told.

I find this generally works and if I see a single magpie I get hassles or, more often, meet up with someone who wants to have a long moan! See if it works for you ...

✦✦ BIRD FLIGHT

If you are looking for an answer to a question, look out for the way birds are flying, to give you an answer.

 Birds flying high – a good omen. If you are looking at a bird and it flies straight up – great!

Direction – flight to the right is a good sign, to the left means delays. A bird flying towards you means happiness is on its way. Away from you may mean your old worries are going, or that there will be some chances that you may miss.

Change of direction – things aren't predictable, someone (maybe you) is likely to change their mind.

Dark and light birds – if there are several shades of bird in a flock, the lighter they are the better the omen. For instance, if a light bird were to fly towards you it would be a better omen than a dark bird.

Bird cries – a bird that sings as it takes flight tells you it's fine to go ahead, but if it cries as it lands you need to be careful. Birds of prey wheeling and screaming are not a good sign and tell you that you will meet a challenge but that you will have the strength to overcome it.

✶✶ CLOUD PICTURES

Want a hint about what's to come? Look into the
clouds! There you will see all sorts of shapes and
you can interpret these in the same way as tea
leaves in a cup (see pages 70–77 for a reminder).

✶✶ FIRE PICTURES

These work in the same way as cloud pictures. In
the old days people always had a real fire burning
 in the hearth and that is something we miss
these days – most of us have no proper fire in
our homes. If you are lucky enough to have
an open fire, gaze into the molten caverns
between the coals and see what you can see. Be
careful not to get too close. Otherwise you can
look into a bonfire – it's one of the exciting
things about November 5th! – or maybe
you have a chimenea that you can use
in the same way. Your parents may
well have a chimenea in the garden.

They are made of cast iron or strong pottery and you can build a fire in them to cook with or just to keep warm when you're outside.

★★ PLANTS

Many native peoples, like the Native Americans, believe that everything is alive and that there is something divine in all that exists. In the Western world our materialism and logic have got in the way of this simple instinct. However, people who work with the hidden and mysterious forces in the Universe do believe that everything is connected in the 'Cosmic Web'. A single plant has a connection with all of its species, all over the earth, and brings with it some particular influences. This is a complicated subject, for each plant is also believed to be ruled by one of the planets. Here we are just going to look at a few easy ways to let plants help us look into the future.

HERBS

Thyme – place some fresh thyme under your pillow to dream of the future.

Basil – to find out how two people will get along, put two basil leaves on a hot surface, like a pan, being very careful as you do it. If the leaves stay still and burn, that's great. If they crackle then there will be some squabbles, and if they fly apart – well sparks may fly!

Rosemary – burn rosemary and smell its smoke to get the answer to a question.

Sage – carry sage to be wise in all you do, including your fortune telling.

FRUIT

Orange – eat an orange thinking of a question with a Yes/No answer. Then count the pips – an even number means no, an odd number means yes.

Apple – cut an apple in half and count the seeds. An even number means you and that lad will soon get together; an odd number means there will be a delay and if one of the seeds is cut, watch out for arguments!

Fig – write a question on a fig leaf – you can just write the initials of the words and it doesn't have to be clear. If the leaf dries slowly it is a good omen, if quickly it's the opposite.

FLOWERS

Daisy – pick a daisy and pull off the petals one by one saying, 'He loves me' with the first petal, 'He loves me not' with the second petal and so on until the last petal, which will tell you whether he does!

Sunflower – sleep with one under your pillow and you will know the truth.

Pansy – plant pansies in a heart shape and if they flourish so will the love that you desire.

Marigolds – it is said that if a girl touches marigolds with bare feet she will understand bird-song.

Lavender – to know if a wish will come true think of it while you put a lavender stalk under your pillow. If you dream about matters connected to your wish then it will be granted.

Rose – to decide which lad to choose, name a green rose leaf for each one. The one that stays

 green the longest gives the answer. (But better still decide you'll be friends with them all anyway!)

This is just a 'taster' of some folk customs that predict the future in nature. However, Nature herself has a message for you. Research has shown that time spent out in parks and fields, near trees and growing things has a much better effect on intuitive powers than sitting in a stuffy, candle-lit room. So if you really want to be a true and wise seer, fresh air is a great teacher!

CHAPTER EIGHT

Your future

In this book we have been looking at lots of ways for you to predict the future and find out what is in store for you and your friends in life. Does this mean that everything is 'mapped out' and that you are in the hands of Fate? No way! Some things are more likely than others, of course, and it is good to know a bit about what lies ahead of you, but the truth is you have many, many choices. One of the most important uses of divination is not to tell you what will happen or what you should do, but to make those choices clear to you.

Another fabulous effect of learning about fortune telling is that it sharpens your intuition. This special sense goes beyond what we learn from our

normal five senses. You can also call it instinct.
Scientists have proved that we do have such
senses by carrying out tests on people.
For instance, if you have your back to
someone and they are staring at you,
something inside you 'knows' and you will find
you often turn and look at the person. This has
 been observed in controlled experiments.
However, people experienced in psychic matters
realize that we are sensitive to much more than
the glances of others, and in fact our minds are
connected to everything around us if we are just
able to open them a little.

Learning about fortune telling is a wonderful way
to extend your awareness. You can access secret
parts of your mind and discover many
exciting things about your own abilities
and also your family, friends and boys
you know. Always remember to be
sensible, to keep your feet on the ground
and to concentrate on positive things.

This way your fortune telling will be not only fun
but also truly helpful to you, guiding
you on your path in life and revealing
to you just how amazing you really are.

Index